EGYPT

NEEDS YOU!

PHARAOHS, SCRIBES,
EMBALMERS, FARMERS,
PRIESTS, TOMB BUILDERS,
SOLDIERS, GOLDSMITHS,
DOCTORS, DANCERS,
ARTISTS, BOATMEN
AND MANY MORE JOBS AVAILABLE
APPLY TO THE VIZIER AT MEMPHIS

ALL IN A DAY'S WORK – PHARAOHS AND EMBALMERS
was produced by **David West** ⚇ **Children's Books,**
5-11 Mortimer Street, LONDON W1N 7RH.

Consultant: Delia Pemberton
Illustrators: Luigi Galante (Virgil Pomfret Agency),
Francis Phillips and Ken Stott (B.L. Kearley Ltd)

First published in Great Britain in 1997 by
Heinemann Children's Reference, an imprint of
Heinemann Educational Publishers, Halley Court,
Jordan Hill, Oxford OX2 8EJ, a division of Reed
Educational and Professional Publishing Limited.

MADRID ATHENS
FLORENCE PRAGUE WARSAW
PORTSMOUTH NH CHICAGO SAO PAULO MEXICO
SINGAPORE TOKYO MELBOURNE AUCKLAND
IBADAN GABORONE JOHANNESBURG KAMPALA
NAIROBI

ISBN 0-431-05380-4 (HB)   ISBN: 0-431-05381-2 (PB)

British Library Cataloguing-In-Publication Data. A
catalogue record for this book is available from the
British Library.

Printed and bound in Italy.
Originated in the UK by RCS Digital Graphics.

ALL · IN · A · DAY'S · WORK

PHARAOHS
AND
EMBALMERS

ANITA GANERI

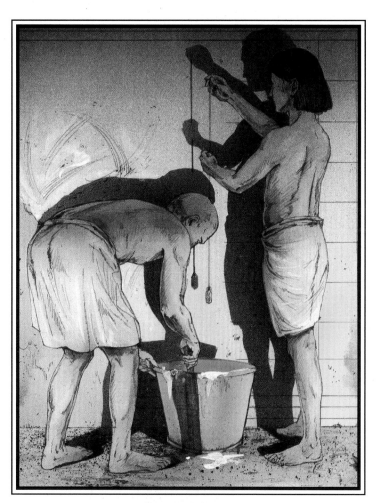

Heinemann

CONTENTS

ANCIENT EGYPTIAN NUMBERS WORK LIKE THIS:			
1	I	1	I
10	∩	2	II
100	୨	3	III
1,000	𓋹	4	IIII
10,000	𓂭	5	IIIII
100,000	𓆐	6	IIIIII
1,000,000	𓁨	7	IIIIIII
		8	IIIIIIII
		9	IIIIIIIII
		10	∩
		11	∩I
		12	∩II
		13	∩III
		14	∩IIII
		15	∩IIIII
		16	∩IIIIII
		17	∩IIIIIII
		18	∩IIIIIIII
		19	∩IIIIIIIII
		20	∩∩
		21	∩∩I
		22	∩∩II
		23	∩∩III
		24	∩∩IIII
		25	∩∩IIIII
		26	∩∩IIIIII
		27	∩∩IIIIIII
		28	∩∩IIIIIIII
		29	∩∩IIIIIIIII
		30	∩∩∩
		31	∩∩∩I
		32	∩∩∩II

INTRODUCTION

Welcome to Ancient Egypt! You've gone back in time 4,000 years and arrived in the greatest civilisation in the ancient world. Take a boat trip along the River Nile to watch the Ancient Egyptians going about their daily lives. A farmer is hard at work in his field. A scribe is writing an official letter. Read on to discover other jobs people did. Will you find the job for you?

YOU COULD COUNT YOURSELF LUCKY if you became Pharaoh, or king. There was no one more important than you. You lived in great luxury, and your word was law. And that wasn't all! To your loyal subjects, you were nothing less than a god on Earth.

PEPI II (2252-2246BC) RULED FOR AN AMAZING 94 YEARS – AND IT'S STILL A WORLD RECORD! WHEN HE DIED, CHAOS BROKE OUT. NO ONE WAS SURE WHO CAME NEXT!

There was no mistaking the Pharaoh. He was the only person allowed to wear the trimmings of royal regalia.

It was rude to call the king by name. That's why he was called 'Pharaoh' which means 'great house'.

JOB DESCRIPTION: THE TOP JOB IN EGYPT. GOD-GIVEN. PERKS INCLUDE POWER, RICHES AND LUXURY ACCOMMODATION.

PAY: BEYOND MEASURE AND TAX FREE.

PHOUR PHAMOUS PHARAOHS

HATSHEPSUT (1490-1468BC)
THE PHARAOH WAS A MAN... USUALLY! QUEEN HATSHEPSUT HAD HERSELF CROWNED 'KING' AND WAS CALLED 'HIS MAJESTY'. SHE EVEN WORE MEN'S CLOTHES (INCLUDING THE FALSE ROYAL BEARD).

TUTANKHAMUN (1347-1337BC)
MAINLY FAMOUS FOR BEING DEAD! HIS TOMB WAS DISCOVERED IN 1922, STUFFED FULL OF GOLD AND TREASURES, INCLUDING HIS MUMMY!

RAMESSES II (1289-1224BC)
ALSO KNOWN AS RAMESSES THE GREAT. GREAT RULER, BUILDER AND WARRIOR. GREAT EGO! HAD MANY GIGANTIC STATUES MADE... OF HIMSELF!

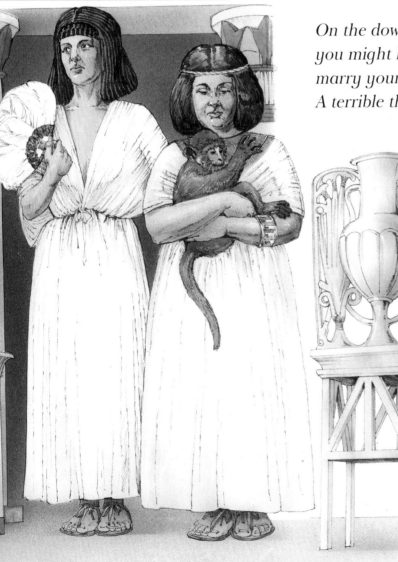

On the down side, you might have to marry your sister. A terrible thought...

DID YOU KNOW?

The Pharaoh was so incredibly important, people thought it an honour to kiss the ground beneath his feet. If you were very lucky, you might get to kiss the royal leg instead!

EGYPTIAN WRITING LOOKED PRETTY but it was very, very tricky to do. Most people couldn't read or write. They hired a scribe to do this for them. Being a scribe was a top job in Ancient Egypt. If you used your brain, fame and fortune were guaranteed.

First, you had to learn to read and write. At about the age of nine, you started scribe school. And there you stayed for the next five to twelve years. The days were long and the teachers strict. They believed that a boy's ears were in his bottom – you had to beat him to make him listen! Woe betide you if you were lazy or disobedient.

Scribes wrote with reed pens dipped in red or black ink. This came in blocks, like poster paints, which you mixed with water or oil.

JOB DESCRIPTION: TOP-NOTCH PROFESSION FOR CAREER-MINDED RECRUITS. SECURE FUTURE PROSPECTS.

PAY: FIRST-CLASS PACKAGE OF PAY AND PERKS.

At scribe school, you copied out texts for hours on end. You practised writing on bits of broken pottery. When you were good enough, and not before, you were allowed to write on a papyrus scroll. (Paper hadn't been invented yet.) You learned to read by chanting texts out loud.

If you were really good, you might become a Vizier, the Pharaoh's Chief Minister. A scribe, called Horemheb, even became Pharaoh.

TOP JOBS FOR SCRIBES

FOR HIGH-FLYING SCRIBES, THE FUTURE WAS ROSY. SCRIBE SCHOOL WAS SIMPLY A STEPPING STONE TO BETTER THINGS:

1. HEAD TEMPLE SCRIBE (IN CHARGE OF THE TEMPLE ACCOUNTS AND WRITING OUT SPELLS AND CHARMS)

2. GOVERNMENT SCRIBE (IN CHARGE OF TAX RETURNS AND OFFICIAL GOVERNMENT REPORTS)

3. SUPERINTENDENT OF DOCUMENTS (CHIEF SCRIBE IN THE LAW COURTS)

4. PERSONAL SCRIBE TO THE COMMANDER OF THE ARMY

5. PERSONAL TUTOR TO A WEALTHY NOBLEMAN

6. HEAD LIBRARIAN IN THE HOUSE OF LIFE (THE TEMPLE LIBRARY)

DID YOU KNOW?

The Egyptians wrote in pictures, called hieroglyphs. This means 'sacred writing'. They believed that writing was a special gift from Thoth, the god of wisdom.

JOBS WANTED

SECOND GOD'S SERVANT
SEEKS POST.
TWO YEARS' EXPERIENCE AT
TEMPLE OF HATHOR.
READING AND WRITING
A SPECIALITY.
ALL OFFERS CONSIDERED.

THE PHARAOH HIMSELF WAS HIGH PRIEST of Egypt. But he was so busy that lesser priests did his duties for him. Each god had a temple which acted as its home on Earth. Only the priests were allowed inside. They looked after the god's statue, feeding and dressing it, as if it were alive. They also prayed, sang and made offerings.

As a priest, you were well respected and could become very powerful. You lived in the temple grounds. Before going on duty, you washed and shaved your head to make you pure. Egyptian priests only worked about one month in three. The rest of the time you went home to your family and returned to your 'regular' job.

JOB DESCRIPTION: HONOURED POSITION IN THE SERVICE OF THE GODS. ACCOMMODATION IN TEMPLE GROUNDS.

PAY: EXCELLENT, WITH SHARE IN TEMPLE INCOME.

MEET THE GODS

2. AMUN-RE
TWO GODS IN ONE – AMUN, CHIEF GOD OF THEBES AND RE. BECAME THE KING OF THE GODS.

4. ISIS
WIFE OF OSIRIS. GODDESS OF CRAFTS. SEEN AS THE PERFECT MOTHER.

1. RE
THE SUN GOD AND CREATOR OF THE WORLD. WAS BORN EVERY MORNING AND DIED EVERY NIGHT.

6. SET
BROTHER OF OSIRIS. GOD OF STORMS AND DESERTS. ALWAYS IN TROUBLE! SHOWN WITH THE HEAD OF A DONKEY OR PIG.

7. ANUBIS
JACKAL-HEADED GOD OF EMBALMING. LED THE DEAD TO OSIRIS'S KINGDOM.

8. BASTET
DAUGHTER OF RE. HAD THE POWER TO MAKE THE CROPS RIPEN. SHOWN AS A CAT.

3. OSIRIS
GOD OF THE DEAD, RULER OF THE UNDERWORLD. SHOWN AS A MUMMIFIED PHARAOH.

5. HORUS
FALCON-HEADED SON OF OSIRIS AND ISIS. A PHARAOH WAS WORSHIPPED AS THE GOD HORUS ON EARTH.

DID YOU KNOW?

If you served as a priest in the Temple of Amun-Re, you might get to wear special leopard skin robes. Otherwise you wore clean, white linen. Wool and leather were not allowed – both were unclean.

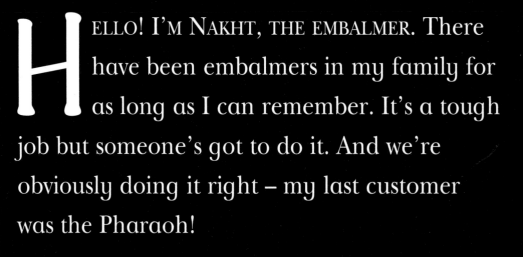

HELLO! I'M NAKHT, THE EMBALMER. There have been embalmers in my family for as long as I can remember. It's a tough job but someone's got to do it. And we're obviously doing it right – my last customer was the Pharaoh!

The Ancient Egyptians were firm believers in life after death. But first you had to make sure your soul survived in the next world.

DID YOU KNOW?

You could even have your pet cat mummified. Not to mention birds, baboons, crocodiles and other sacred creatures. Or you could buy a ready-wrapped animal mummy to offer to the gods!

JOB DESCRIPTION: REGULAR WORK. REQUIRES TACT AND SYMPATHY. STRONG STOMACH A MUST.

PAY: EXCELLENT REWARDS FOR A MUMMY WELL DONE.

This wouldn't happen if your body was left to rot away. And so you were mummified to make you last!

Being an embalmer was a very good job. If you worked hard, you could become Chief Embalmer. Then you might get to wear a splendid jackal mask (because Anubis, the Egyptian god of embalmers, was shown with a jackal's head).

MAKING A MUMMY

1. THE EMBALMER TAKES THE BODY TO HIS WORKSHOP WHICH IS CALLED 'THE BEAUTIFUL HOUSE'!

2. A CUT IS MADE IN THE LEFT SIDE AND THE INSIDES ARE TAKEN OUT. THESE ARE STORED IN SPECIAL JARS. THEN THE BRAIN'S PULLED OUT THROUGH THE NOSE.

3. THE BODY IS PACKED IN A KIND OF SALT TO DRY IT OUT. THIS TAKES ABOUT 40 DAYS.

4. TO MAKE IT MORE LIFE-LIKE, THE BODY IS PADDED WITH LINEN AND SAWDUST.

5. THEN IT'S WRAPPED IN LINEN BANDAGES, WITH LUCKY CHARMS TUCKED BETWEEN THE LAYERS.

6. A DEATH MASK, PAINTED TO LOOK LIKE THE PERSON, IS PLACED OVER THE MUMMY'S HEAD.

7. FINALLY, THE MUMMY IS PUT IN A COFFIN.

W ITH A GOOD BEDSIDE MANNER and an ear for a problem, you might have become a doctor. Egyptian doctors were the best in the ancient world. They couldn't cure everyone, but their skills and knowledge were the best around.

Watching the embalmers at work taught them a lot about the human body.

I f a patient came to see you, complaining of a headache (the Egyptians called it 'half-head'), you examined them and asked them questions. Their diet was particularly important. Doctors blamed many ailments on over-eating! You gave a prescription and made notes. Your notes were useful for future cases.

JOB DESCRIPTION: CAREER IN CARING PROFESSION. YOU'VE GOT TO WANT TO DO IT.

PAY: VERY GOOD RATES IF THOSE CURES KEEP COMING.

Egyptian doctors had medical textbooks full of treatments for illnesses ranging from toothache to cures for making old people look younger. Many remedies were made from plants and herbs. These were given out in little, labelled bottles, much as they are today.

If all else failed, you could always pray for a miracle. If you couldn't cure a snake bite with medicine, a magic spell might just do the trick. Some people spent the night in the temple in the hope that the gods would show them a cure in their dreams.

Some doctors specialised in eyes and teeth. Dentists filled rich people's teeth with gold.

DID YOU KNOW?

The Egyptians believed that many diseases were caused by worm-like creatures getting into the body. They also suffered from terrible feet because they very rarely wore shoes. Snakebites, scorpion stings and crocodile bites were daily hazards.

MOST ORDINARY EGYPTIANS worked as farmers, growing crops such as barley, grapes, pomegranates, beans and cucumbers. If you were lucky, you might have your own field. But most people worked for wealthy nobles or on temple estates. You paid them taxes out of your crops. You paid taxes to the Pharaoh too.

Without the River Nile, nothing could grow in Ancient Egypt. Most of the country was desert (thought to be full of demons). Every year the river flooded, covering its banks with thick, black mud – perfect for growing things in! The river also watered the fields.

JOB DESCRIPTION: SEASONAL WORK IN THE GREAT OUTDOORS. GOOD, HONEST TOIL.

PAY: PAID BY THE BASKETFUL.

DID YOU KNOW?

Barley was made into bread and beer, the main part of your diet. Egyptian bread was full of grit and tough to chew. Beer was thick and lumpy. It was strained, then sipped through a straw.

Many farmers kept cattle, ducks and geese. The River Nile was full of fish. Meat was very expensive.

THE FARMER'S YEAR

FLOOD SEASON (JULY – NOVEMBER)
NO FARMING TO DO WHILE THE RIVER FLOODS. YOU'RE SENT TO WORK ON THE PHARAOH'S NEW TOMB.
WEEK OFF – TIME TO RELAX BEFORE IT GETS BUSY.
P.S. DON'T FORGET TO GIVE THANKS TO HAPI (THE GOD WHO MAKES THE RIVER FLOOD).

GROWING SEASON (DECEMBER – MARCH)
FLOODS FALLING BACK. IT'S ALL GO NOW. TIME TO PLOUGH THE LAND AND SOW THE SEEDS. YOUR HERDS FOLLOW BEHIND AND TRAMPLE THE SEEDS IN.
YOU'RE KEPT VERY BUSY, WEEDING AND WATERING... AND THROWING STONES AT THE PESKY BIRDS!

HARVEST TIME (MARCH – JULY)
YOU HARVEST THE GRAIN WITH A SHARP SICKLE. IT'S TIED IN BUNDLES AND LOADED INTO BASKETS AND ON TO THE BACK OF A DONKEY. THEN IT'S SORTED AND STORED. THE TAX COLLECTOR WORKS OUT HOW MUCH TAX YOU HAVE TO PAY.
NOW ALL THAT'S LEFT IS TO REPAIR THE CANALS (WHICH BRING WATER FROM THE RIVER) AND MEND YOUR TOOLS, READY FOR NEXT YEAR.

NAME: IMHOTEP
OCCUPATION: ROYAL ARCHITECT
CLAIM TO FAME: DESIGNED AND BUILT THE VERY FIRST PYRAMID IN ABOUT 2600BC.
EDUCATION: SCRIBE SCHOOL, THEN COLLEGE OF ARCHITECTS. ALSO NATURALLY BRILLIANT.
OTHER HOBBIES AND SKILLS: VIZIER (CHIEF MINISTER); CHIEF PRIEST; DOCTOR; MATHEMATICIAN; SAID TO HAVE INVENTED THE CALENDAR; GOD (AFTER HIS DEATH, HE WAS WORSHIPPED FOR BEING SO WISE).

EVEN WHEN YOUR FIELDS FLOODED you didn't have time to rest. You had to enrol in the royal workforce as part of the tax you owed to the Pharaoh. There was no getting out of it – new temples and tombs always needed to be built.

JOB DESCRIPTION: BACK-BREAKING WORK. MANY WEEKS SPENT AWAY FROM HOME.

PAY: NONE. THIS IS PART OF THE TAX YOU OWE TO THE PHARAOH.

The most famous tombs were pyramids, built for the Pharaohs and their families. They were buried with masses of gold, jewels, furniture, statues, even models of servants – everything they needed in the next world. These were rich pickings for tomb robbers. So later tombs were cut deep into the cliffs for safety. It didn't work! These were robbed, too.

DID YOU KNOW?

The name 'pyramid' may have come from a Greek word for 'wheat cake'. This was because the pyramids were shaped like a type of little cake eaten in Greece.

BUILD YOUR OWN PYRAMID

1. FIRST, THE PHARAOH SUMMONS THE ARCHITECT TO DISCUSS HIS PLANS.

2. THEN THE SURVEYORS MARK OUT A PERFECT SQUARE FOR THE BASE.

3. THE GROUND IS CLEARED OF SAND AND STONE.

4. BUILDING BEGINS. THE PYRAMID IS BUILT IN GIANT STEPS, USING MASSIVE STONE BLOCKS CUT AND FERRIED IN FROM A QUARRY IN THE DESERT. THESE ARE HAULED INTO PLACE UP A HUGE MUD RAMP. IT'S VERY HARD WORK.

5. THE CAPSTONE GOES ON TOP.

6. THE WHOLE PYRAMID IS COVERED IN WHITE LIMESTONE BLOCKS. THESE ARE HUGE TOO!

7. WORKERS USE ROUNDED STONES TO BASH AND RUB THE OUTER LAYER UNTIL IT IS SMOOTH.

8. AT LAST, YOUR WORK IS DONE. YOU'RE GLAD TO BE GOING HOME. BUT YOU'LL BE BACK – MORE PYRAMIDS ARE ALWAYS NEEDED.

THE EGYPTIAN ARMY NEEDS YOU!

RECRUITS URGENTLY NEEDED FOR NEW CAMPAIGN. PREVIOUS EXPERIENCE NOT REQUIRED. TRAINING GIVEN.

CONTACT:
GENERAL AHMOSE
PTAH DIVISION

T HE EGYPTIANS WERE NOT GREAT FIGHTERS. They didn't really need to be. For much of their history, they lived in peace with their neighbours. But times changed. To drive out invaders and conquer new lands, the Egyptians made their army bigger, stronger and better organised, with the Pharaoh at its head.

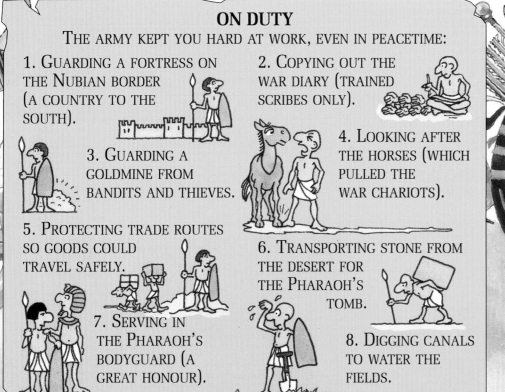

ON DUTY

THE ARMY KEPT YOU HARD AT WORK, EVEN IN PEACETIME:

1. GUARDING A FORTRESS ON THE NUBIAN BORDER (A COUNTRY TO THE SOUTH).

2. COPYING OUT THE WAR DIARY (TRAINED SCRIBES ONLY).

3. GUARDING A GOLDMINE FROM BANDITS AND THIEVES.

4. LOOKING AFTER THE HORSES (WHICH PULLED THE WAR CHARIOTS).

5. PROTECTING TRADE ROUTES SO GOODS COULD TRAVEL SAFELY.

6. TRANSPORTING STONE FROM THE DESERT FOR THE PHARAOH'S TOMB.

7. SERVING IN THE PHARAOH'S BODYGUARD (A GREAT HONOUR).

8. DIGGING CANALS TO WATER THE FIELDS.

If you liked adventure, the army was the place for you. High-ranking officers became famous and rich. Ordinary soldiers trained and worked hard. But if they fought bravely, they might be rewarded with gifts of land and with slaves. Not to mention a share of any gold or loot captured from the enemy.

The bravest soldiers were awarded gold medals in the shape of flies.

DID YOU KNOW?

To keep count of how many enemy soldiers they'd killed, the Egyptians cut off their hands. At the end of a battle, the army scribe totted up the total.

THE ANCIENT EGYPTIANS LOVED JEWELLERY. If you were poor, copper rings and glass beads were all you could afford. But if you were rich, the sky was the limit. You wore fabulous necklaces, rings and bracelets of gold, inlaid with semi-precious stones. Gold amulets (lucky charms) were all the rage.

All this was good news for goldsmiths. You were kept hard at work, producing exquisite pieces that sold for a fortune. Usually the gold was beaten into shape with a stone, or melted, then poured into a mould and left to harden. As an extra-special touch, tiny beadlets of gold were soldered on to the finished thing.

If your father was a goldsmith, you followed in his footsteps.

JOB DESCRIPTION: HIGHLY SKILLED AND DELICATE WORK. MUST KEEP UP WITH THE LATEST FASHIONS.

PAY: GREAT POSSIBILITIES. THE FINEST PIECES SELL LIKE HOT CAKES.

EIGHT GREAT EGYPTIAN CRAFTS

1. BEAD MAKER
BEADS ARE MADE FROM TINY PIECES OF SEMI-PRECIOUS STONES WITH A HOLE DRILLED THROUGH THEM. THEY MAKE GREAT JEWELLERY.

2. LEATHER WORKER
LEATHER IS WORKED INTO SHIELDS, SANDALS, CHEAP FURNITURE AND ARMOUR.

3. BASKET WEAVER
BASKETS ARE WOVEN FROM REEDS, RUSHES OR PALM LEAVES. THEY'RE GOOD FOR STORING AND CARRYING THINGS.

4. PAPYRUS MAKER
SCRIBES WRITE ON SHEETS OF PAPYRUS, MADE OF BEATEN REEDS. SEVERAL SHEETS ARE STUCK TOGETHER TO MAKE A SCROLL.

5. FURNITURE MAKER
THE FINEST FURNITURE IS MADE OF BEST QUALITY EBONY AND CEDAR, INLAID WITH IVORY, GOLD LEAF AND SEMI-PRECIOUS STONES.

6. IVORY CARVER
IVORY COMES FROM ELEPHANT AND HIPPO TUSKS. THOUGHT TO HAVE MAGICAL POWERS, IT'S CARVED INTO KNIVES, SPOONS AND BUTTONS.

8. METALSMITH
OTHER SMITHS WORK IN COPPER, SILVER AND BRONZE, MAKING TOOLS, WEAPONS AND JEWELLERY. SILVER IS RARER AND MORE PRECIOUS THAN GOLD.

7. POTTER
POTTERS MAKE COOKING POTS, STORAGE JARS AND DRINKING CUPS.

DID YOU KNOW?
On special occasions, the Pharaoh would shower his faithful servants with precious necklaces. This was to reward outstanding service to the state.

YOU ARE CORDIALLY
INVITED TO THE OPENING
OF THE NEW
TOMB GALLERY

ENTRANCE FREE
BROWSERS AND
BUYERS WELCOME

ARTISTS AND SCULPTORS were much in demand in Ancient Egypt to produce paintings and sculptures for temples and tombs. So, if you were good at art, with a steady hand and an eye for colour, and you didn't mind the years of training, this could be the job for you. If you were very good, you'd soon be snapped up by the Pharaoh.

PAINTING A PICTURE

1. You cover the wall with plaster to make it level.

2. When the plaster's dry, you mark out a grid on the wall, in red.

3. Then you draw the outlines of the picture, also in red.

4. Your supervisor corrects these in black. (This is the worst part!)

JOB DESCRIPTION: THE PERFECT JOB FOR THE CREATIVE MIND. PRIDE IN YOUR WORK ESSENTIAL.

PAY: TOP RATES PAID FOR TRUE WORKS OF ART.

In Egyptian art important people were drawn as large figures and lesser people were shown small.

The walls of tombs were covered in pictures. Many showed scenes from everyday life. The Egyptians believed that these scenes had magical powers. For example, pictures of people bringing food and drink meant that you wouldn't go hungry in the afterlife.

DID YOU KNOW?

The Pharaoh was painted to look strong, handsome and manly. Even if he wasn't!

5. Then you fill in the colours...

6. ... and the details, such as the eyes.

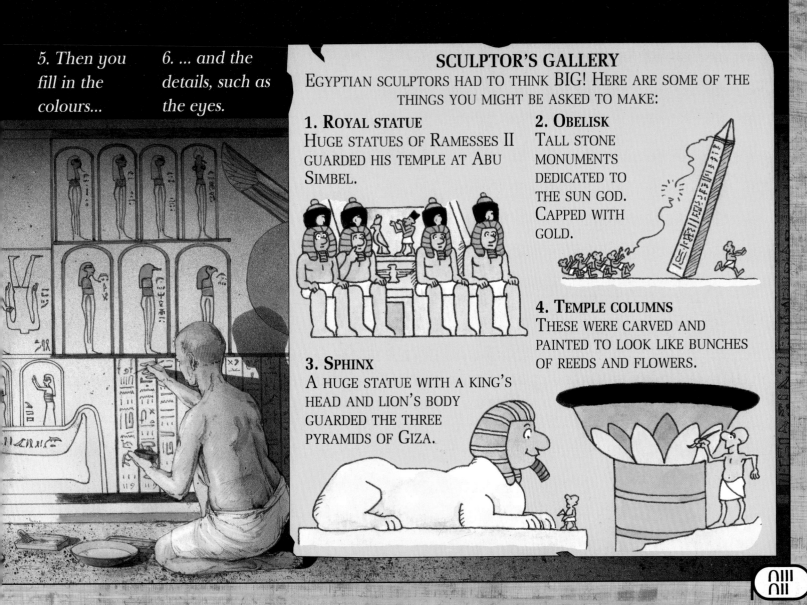

SCULPTOR'S GALLERY

EGYPTIAN SCULPTORS HAD TO THINK BIG! HERE ARE SOME OF THE THINGS YOU MIGHT BE ASKED TO MAKE:

1. ROYAL STATUE
HUGE STATUES OF RAMESSES II GUARDED HIS TEMPLE AT ABU SIMBEL.

2. OBELISK
TALL STONE MONUMENTS DEDICATED TO THE SUN GOD. CAPPED WITH GOLD.

3. SPHINX
A HUGE STATUE WITH A KING'S HEAD AND LION'S BODY GUARDED THE THREE PYRAMIDS OF GIZA.

4. TEMPLE COLUMNS
THESE WERE CARVED AND PAINTED TO LOOK LIKE BUNCHES OF REEDS AND FLOWERS.

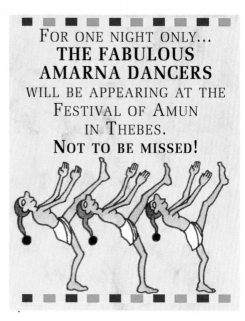

Women were quite well treated in Ancient Egypt. They could own their own land and earn their own living. Many women would marry young and stay at home to look after their families. (The Ancient Egyptians loved children!) But some worked.

If you were fast on your feet, you might have joined a dance troupe. Dancers performed at religious festivals and were hired to entertain guests at parties and banquets. They were accompanied by singers and musicians, playing flutes, harps and castanets.

We don't know what Egyptian music sounded like. But it probably had a strong beat because listeners liked to clap along.

DID YOU KNOW?

One thing women didn't have to do was the washing. It was much too dangerous because of all the hungry crocodiles lurking in the river!

It was even better if you could turn somersaults. Acrobats were in great demand!

OTHER JOBS FOR WOMEN

IF THE WORLD OF SHOWBUSINESS WASN'T FOR YOU, THERE WERE VARIOUS OTHER JOBS YOU COULD TRY:

1. ROYAL HEIRESS
THE ELDEST DAUGHTER OF THE KING AND QUEEN. YOUR JOB IS TO MARRY THE NEXT KING AND BECOME QUEEN.

3. MOURNER
PROFESSIONAL MOURNERS ARE HIRED TO FOLLOW THE COFFINS OF RICH EGYPTIANS. THEY WEEP AND WAIL, AND TEAR AT THEIR HAIR.

5. LANDLADY
IF THEIR HUSBANDS ARE AWAY, WEALTHY EGYPTIAN WOMEN TAKE OVER THE RUNNING OF THEIR FARMS AND ESTATES.

7. WIG-MAKER
WEALTHY EGYPTIAN MEN AND WOMEN WEAR BLACK WIGS, MADE OF WOOL OR SOMETIMES OF REAL HUMAN HAIR.

9. MIDWIFE
SOME TEMPLES RUN MEDICAL SCHOOLS WHERE WOMEN CAN TRAIN AS MIDWIVES.

2. PERFUME MAKER
PERFUME IS POPULAR IN ANCIENT EGYPT. AT BANQUETS, GUESTS WEAR CONES OF PERFUMED WAX ON THEIR HEADS. THEY'RE COOL AND REFRESHING AS THEY MELT.

4. WEAVER
YOU ARE KEPT VERY BUSY, WEAVING LINEN FOR CLOTHES, AND FOR BANDAGES TO WRAP ALL THOSE MUMMIES IN!

6. MAID
YOU MIGHT WORK AS A SERVANT IN A WEALTHY FAMILY. YOU HELP WITH ALL THE HOUSEHOLD CHORES AND LOOK AFTER YOUR MISTRESS'S NEEDS.

8. PRIESTESS
GIRLS FROM GOOD FAMILIES CAN BECOME PRIESTESSES IN ONE OF THE MANY TEMPLES.

10. AND FINALLY... PHARAOH
REMEMBER 'HIS' MAJESTY, QUEEN HATSHEPSUT? (SEE PAGE ||||||) BUT FEW WOMEN MADE IT TO THE VERY TOP.

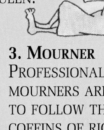

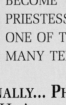

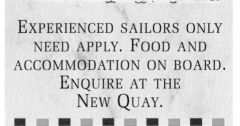

M ESSING ABOUT ON THE RIVER was second nature to an Ancient Egyptian. People went everywhere by boat. If you liked sailing, there were plenty of jobs to choose. You might be a ferryman, rowing passengers across the Nile. Or you could become one of a crew of 40 on board a royal barge.

A BOAT-SPOTTER'S GUIDE

1. FISHING BOAT
MADE OF BUNDLES OF REEDS AND ROWED ALONG. ALSO USED AS A FERRY. LATER MADE OF WOOD.

2. SAILING BOAT
SAILS WERE INVENTED ABOUT 5,000 YEARS AGO (BY THE ANCIENT EGYPTIANS, OF COURSE).

3. FUNERAL BARGE
CARRIED THE BODIES OF WEALTHY PEOPLE DOWN THE NILE TO THEIR TOMBS.

JOB DESCRIPTION: OUTDOOR LIFE WITH OPPORTUNITIES FOR FOREIGN TRAVEL. KNOWLEDGE OF BOATS A MUST.

PAY: VARIES — IT DEPENDS ON THE TYPE OF VOYAGE.

Y ou might never go much further. Most Ancient Egyptians weren't keen on travel. After all, when you lived in the most beautiful, most sophisticated land in the world, what was the point of leaving it? Egyptian merchants sailed north up the Nile and out into the Mediterranean Sea. But most people preferred to stay comfortably at home.

DID YOU KNOW?

Boats were so important in Ancient Egypt that people believed the gods used them too. Even the mighty sun god, Re, made his daily journey across the sky by boat. By night, he sailed through the underworld.

4. MERCHANT SHIP

CARRIED GOODS AND MERCHANTS TO AND FROM EGYPT, VIA THE MEDITERRANEAN AND THE RED SEA.

5. CARGO BARGE

USED TO TRANSPORT HEAVY GOODS, SUCH AS STATUES AND BUILDING STONES, UP AND DOWN THE NILE.

6. WARSHIP

BUILT FOR RARE SEA BATTLES, SUCH AS WHEN RAMESSES II DEFEATED THE SEA PEOPLES AND SAVED EGYPT.

GLOSSARY

Amulet

A lucky charm worn to give protection from illnesses and evil spirits.

Embalmer

A person who prepared a dead body for burial. The embalmer wrapped the body in bandages to make a mummy.

Hieroglyphs

Egyptian writing which used pictures for words and sounds. It was very tricky to read and write. Most Egyptians didn't learn how to.

Horemheb

Horemheb trained as a scribe and had a successful career in the army. He became Pharaoh after the death of Ay, who was Tutankhamun's successor.

Imhotep

A royal architect, believed to have built the first-ever pyramid in Egypt in about 2600BC. A very clever man who is reputed to have invented the calendar too.

Linen

A fine cloth made from the fibres of the flax plant. Most Egyptians wore linen clothes.

Mummy

A body which had been prepared and wrapped in bandages, ready for burial.

Obelisk

A tall stone pillar with a pointed top, dedicated to the sun god. The sides were carved with dedications to the gods and to Pharaoh.

Papyrus

A type of reed which grew along the River Nile. Sails, mats, boats and writing materials were all made from papyrus.

Pyramid

A huge, stone tomb built for the Pharaoh. The Great Pyramid at Giza, built for King Khufu, is one of the Wonders of the World.

Scribe

A person employed to write and copy texts and letters. Scribes were highly trained and very well paid.

Sphinx

A statue which usually had the body of a lion with the head of a king, hawk or ram. Used to guard temples and pyramids.

Vizier

The two Viziers were the Pharaoh's chief ministers and the most important officials in the country. They carried out the Pharaoh's orders and collected taxes.

1	I	9	IIIIIIIII	17	∩IIIIIII	25	∩∩IIIII
2	II	10	∩	18	∩IIIIIIII	26	∩∩IIIIII
3	III	11	∩I	19	∩IIIIIIIII	27	∩∩IIIIIII
4	IIII	12	∩II	20	∩∩	28	∩∩IIIIIIII
5	IIIII	13	∩III	21	∩∩I	29	∩∩IIIIIIIII
6	IIIIII	14	∩IIII	22	∩∩II	30	∩∩∩
7	IIIIIII	15	∩IIIII	23	∩∩III	31	∩∩∩I
8	IIIIIIII	16	∩IIIIII	24	∩∩IIII	32	∩∩∩II